Contents

Above left: A simple farmhouse stands surrounded by emerald green rice fields in northern Luzon.

Top right: A dancer strikes a pose at the end of his performance, at Dinagyang Festival, in Iloilo.

Above: The 'banca', or pump-boat, is the classic Philippine inter-island mode of transport, seen here in Bohol.

Chapter 1: A Pacific Rim Archipelago

Dreams of a tropical island escape inevitably conjure up visions of blinding white sands lined by swaying palm trees, perhaps framed by a backdrop of rugged cloud-capped mountains, the sand lapped by a crystal-clear azure sea. Beneath the water's perfectly white-tipped waves lie spectacularly colourful coral reefs populated by shoals of iridescent fish of all shapes and sizes, an occasional frisson of excitement thrown into an otherwise blissfully relaxing scene by the shadow of a passing shark.

Below: Typically rugged mountains of northern Luzon, partly cloaked in forest, partly turned over to agriculture, cut into steep rice terraces.

Such dreams could easily serve as a description of the Philippines, or at least significant numbers of its 7,000-plus islands. Admittedly, to describe the whole of this island nation as a tropical paradise would be an exaggeration, but so many of its sandy, palm-lined beaches and islands match our 'Robinson Crusoe-esque' imaginings that they almost seem like a dream come true. Couple this with an unwaveringly enthusiastic and friendly welcome from the locals and it is easy to see how the Philippines rates as one of the world's great tropical island getaways.

Not that the Philippines is about only beaches, coral reefs and sparkling seas, of course. Inland rise some of

Southeast Asia's most rugged mountain ranges, many of them volcanic, some still cloaked in dense tropical rainforest. They are home to a huge diversity of plant and animal wildlife seen nowhere else on Earth. It is for good reason that scientists have classified the Philippines as one of the world's nine priceless biodiversity hotspots.

Diversity continues at the human level, though initially the country can appear to be ethnically rather uniform. However, this superficial impression masks a diverse and widespread range of peoples, particularly in the remote mountainous regions of the north, among the Muslim groups of the far south and across some of the remoter island groups. It adds up to a great human variety that lends an extra dimension of fascination to an already beautiful and vibrant country.

Top: The stunning Seven Commandos Beach is typical of the many sandy bays, accessible only by boat, scattered around the islands of El Nido, in northern Palawan.

Above: A Melithaea species sea fan thriving on one of the Philippines' many coral reefs, this one is the remote Tubbataha Reef, off the coast of Palawan.

Philippine Landscapes

When viewed on a map, it is easy to see that the Philippines is a tightly packed cluster of islands (though they can feel anything but tightly packed when travelling among them by boat!), forming part of a massive island chain that stretches all the way from Kamchatka on the southern coast of Siberia down to the northern tip of Australia. Together they form the western arc of the Pacific Rim. In the case of the Philippines, not only do its islands form a chunk of the Pacific's western shore but they also constitute a very large proportion of the eastern border of the largely land-encircled South China Sea, shielding much of mainland Southeast Asia from the Pacific Ocean. In forming that shield, the Philippines is a long country running north-south, reaching to within 200 km (125 miles) of Taiwan in the far north and stretching down almost as far as the islands of eastern Indonesia in the far south, a distance of some 2,000 km (1,250 miles).

Left: *A view across Puerto Galera, in northern Mindoro, showing a highly indented and island-studded coastline, typical of much of the Philippines.*

Left: *Sunset across the remote rugged islands of El Nido, on the northeast coast of Palawan and bordering the South China Sea.*

Below left: *A coconut palm leans across the sandy shore of Guyam, a tiny island protected from the nearby Pacific surf by its position among the Siargao Islands, a little archipelago off the northeast coast of Mindanao.*

There are five main island groups, namely Luzon, Mindanao, the Visayas, Mindoro and Palawan. Luzon, lying in the north, is the Philippines' largest island, with Mindanao (in the far south) coming a close second. Together, they occupy about half of the country's land area. The Visayas is a fractured mass of small islands that make up the Philippines' central belt, while Mindoro is a large, but still quite remote, island nestling close to Luzon's southwest coast. Palawan, the wildest and least developed of the Philippines' regions, is a very long, almost pencil-thin island group lying some way to the west of the main body of the Philippines. It runs from a short distance west of Mindoro south-westwards for nearly 700 km (about 430 miles) and ends barely 60 km (about 37 miles) from Borneo.

The country's reputation for dazzling tropical beaches and coral reefs largely derives from the islands of Palawan and the Visayas, which attract the majority of visitors in search of sand- and sun-blessed coasts.

A Volcanic and Seismic Landscape

An alternative name for the Pacific Rim is the Ring of Fire, since the entire island chain from Kamchatka down to Indonesia is highly volcanic. With many hundreds of volcanoes dotting the landscape, 22 of them presently known to be active, the Philippines is a fully paid-up member of this club. Much of the landscape is characterized by these volcanoes, their slopes sweeping up in graceful curves, gently at first but then ever steeper towards the summit, towering ominously above the surrounding countryside or coast.

Arguably the most spectacular of these is Mount Mayon, an almost perfect 'textbook' conical volcano looming above the city of Legazpi in southern Luzon. Unfortunately, it is also the liveliest, experiencing regular, but relatively small, eruptions every few years. The biggest and deadliest eruption

Above: *The shattered and flooded crater of Mount Pinatubo, seen over a decade after its massive 1991 eruption.*

Below: *Mount Mayon, the Philippines' most active volcano, towers threateningly above the city of Legazpi, in southern Luzon.*

Left: Ardent Hot Springs, a popular bathing spot on the slopes of Mount Hibok-Hibok, an active volcano on Camiguin Island, off the north coast of Mindanao, is one of the benign gifts of a volcanic landscape.

Below: Seen from the rim of the Taal caldera, the little Taal Volcano, sitting on an island in Lake Taal, looks quite innocuous. In fact, it is one of the Philippines' most dangerous volcanoes.

in recent times, however, was that of Pinatubo, in northern Luzon, which exploded with devastating effect in 1991 after lying dormant for over 400 years.

Fortunately, however, most of the time the volcanoes simply lend a dramatic, and often stunningly beautiful, aspect to the landscape. They are natural features to be admired and explored, although they should always also be treated with respect and some caution.

All this volcanism is closely linked to the immense seismic activity that rumbles under the Philippines, which is the result of huge tectonic forces at work in the Earth's crust. The country sits on its own relatively small tectonic plate, which is gradually being crushed between the very much larger Eurasian and Australasian plates, steadily pushing the islands ever upwards. The result is a characteristically mountainous landscape criss-crossed by fault lines and pockmarked with volcanoes. The highest peaks reach nearly 3,000 m (9,840 ft), the tallest of them being Mount Apo at 2,956 m (9,698 ft), an inactive volcano in southern Mindanao.

Right: The instantly recognizable Pompadour Green-Pigeon, 'Treron pompadora', is quite a common resident of many Philippine forests, particularly at the forest edges.

Below: A young Philippine Deer, 'Rusa marianna', a species spread thinly across much of the Philippines.

Right: This tangle of vegetation in dense rainforest, in El Nido, Palawan, is typical of the Philippines' natural vegetation, as it would be across much of the country were it not for human activity.

Left: The Philippine Tarsier, 'Tarsius syrichta', at 8 cm (3 in) long is one of the world's smallest primates. It is unique to Bohol and Mindanao but is related to a tarsier in Borneo.

Below: A typical rural scene, a stream flowing through verdant forest as it drops down out of the mountainous interior. Seen on the slopes of Mount Hibok-Hibok, on Camiguin Island, Mindanao.

Above: A gigantic tree surrounded by bamboo, growing in lowland rainforest in Subic Bay, northern Luzon.

A Unique Natural Environment

Having been driven up from the ocean floor by tectonic movement, most of the Philippine islands have never formed part of any of the world's major landmasses. As a result, a significant proportion of the Philippines' plant and animal wildlife has evolved in glorious isolation, resulting in an immense diversity of species found nowhere else. Only Palawan is an exception to this rule, a land bridge having once joined it to Borneo, giving it a fauna and flora related to this part of Southeast Asia. Even within the Philippines, the various island groups have remained isolated from each other for so long that different, though related, species have evolved in each.

Below: The Philippine Eagle, 'Pithecophaga jefferyi', is the king of the Philippine rainforest. At over 1 m (39 in) tall and with a wingspan of 2 m (6½ ft), it is one of the world's largest eagles.

Life in the Rainforest

As a wholly tropical country, tropical rainforest is the natural vegetation for pretty well the entire country, even at high altitude, and it is likely that at one time almost the whole of the Philippines was forested. Not surprisingly, the vast majority of the country's 12,000-plus plant species (including nearly 4,000 species of native tree) make up this environment, while the bulk of its animal wildlife is adapted to life in the Philippine rainforest.

Over 600 species of birds have been found in the Philippines, the great majority living in the forests, more than 190 of them unique to the country. Many are quite small and difficult to spot among the vegetation, but the largest and most spectacular is the magnificent Philippine Eagle, standing over 1 m (39 in) tall and with a wingspan of over 2 m (6½ ft), making it the world's second largest eagle.

An even higher proportion of the less mobile animal species are endemic. Three-quarters of the 190-plus species of mammal, for instance, are unique to the Philippines. Only one of the well known primates typically found across

Left: The Long-tailed or Crab-eating Macaque, 'Macaca fascicularis', is widely found in Philippine rainforests and is one of the few large mammals to have made the jump from mainland Asia to the Philippine islands.

Below: Huge fruit-bats, here seen roosting in a tree in rainforest in Subic Bay, northern Luzon, commonly live in mixed species colonies. They are widespread in Philippine lowland forests.

Southeast Asia is found in the Philippines and that is the Crab-eating or Long-tailed Macaque, which is frequently seen in forests across much of the country. Another primate that, though endemic, is related to one found in Borneo is the Philippine Tarsier. This tiny, cute animal, with a body barely 8 cm (3 in) long and a tail nearly twice that, is restricted to forests in Bohol and Mindanao.

The largest of the Philippines' endemic mammals is undoubtedly the Tamaraw, a shy dwarf buffalo found only on Mindoro. By contrast, the great majority of the country's mammals are quite small and inconspicuous. There are, for instance, many types of cloud rats, a rodent that exists as a number of species with very limited ranges in specific parts of the country. About 20 per cent of all the country's mammals are bats, ranging from tiny, hard-to-see insect-eaters up to enormous fruit-eating species with wingspans of almost 2 m (6½ ft). They are frequently seen roosting as large colonies in their favourite rainforest trees.

Life in the Sea

Things couldn't be more different in the sea. Dive near any healthy coral reef and you are immediately surrounded by a cornucopia of animal life, not just the corals themselves, of course, but also a huge range of fish species. These creatures are not restricted to the Philippines as many of the land animals are; all the marine life found here is distributed across much of the Indo-Pacific region, from the tiniest coral species to the largest shark or whale.

Indeed, with 500-plus species of coral found in Philippine, Indonesian and Malaysian waters, this region may be the primary source of the corals found across much of the Indian and Pacific Oceans. Mobile marine life is no less diverse, the nooks and crannies of a reef providing a home for a great range of invertebrates, such as shrimps, crabs, lobsters and squid, while the surrounding waters are filled with an enormous stock of fish ranging from tiny, brightly coloured clownfish up to tuna, sharks and the occasional manta ray.

Above: Sea fans are corals commonly found in the deeper waters around Philippine reefs, particularly on steep walls where currents are strong. This one is a 'Melithaea' species, seen on Tubbataha Reef, off the coast of Palawan.

Left: A typical scene on the crest of a coral reef, showing a dense mixture of different species of hard and soft corals. Seen on Tubbataha Reef, off the coast of Palawan.

Threats and Conservation

Commercial exploitation and a burgeoning human population have taken a heavy toll on the Philippines' natural environment. Forest cover is probably little more than 10 per cent of what it was 100 years ago and much of what survives is badly damaged. This loss of habitat has put not only a large number of endemic plants on the endangered species lists but also many forest-living animals. Foremost among these is the mighty Philippine Eagle, now probably restricted to just a few hundred survivors in the wild, scattered across Mindanao and northeast Luzon, plus the islands of Samar and Leyte.

The Philippines developed one of Southeast Asia's first protected areas systems, established by the American colonial government during the early years of the 20th century, but after independence, gained in 1946, this initiative was largely ignored. Many supposedly protected areas were heavily logged and then settled by farmers. From the late 1980s onwards, plans were set in motion to rescue the situation, a number of internationally funded and organized programmes being set up, aimed at rejuvenating the protected areas system and safeguarding the best and largest of the remaining wild areas.

A number of home-grown environmental conservation movements also gained momentum, principally the Haribon Foundation and the Philippine Eagle Foundation (PEF). The latter took upon itself the task of saving the Philippine Eagle, initiating the first attempts at captive breeding, as well as undertaking conservation work in Mindanao's forests. For some time captive breeding proved to be almost impossible, but in recent years there has been considerable success and PEF is now engaged in experimental releases of captively bred eagles back into the wild.

As on land, the marine environment is also in trouble. Most reefs are seriously damaged by over-fishing, pollution and the indiscriminate use of dynamite (to catch fish quickly). However, conservation measures are now having an impact. Reefs that have been long-protected either as

Top: Fishermen, such as those seen here on Camiguin Island, Mindanao, have been finding it increasingly difficult to catch enough fish to support themselves.

Above: A replanted and steadily recovering mangrove swamp in Subic Bay, Luzon, points to increasing efforts to restore the Philippines' environment.

important tourist diving or university research sites continue in good health, while regeneration is starting to take place at those environments included in protected areas programmes. Instigation in the 1990s of small, highly localized marine reserves specifically aimed at protecting reefs to boost fish stocks initially met stiff resistance from local fishermen. However, so successful were they in achieving their goals that fishing communities right across the country are now increasingly organizing their own reserves.

The People

The Philippines' almost 100 million people must be among the friendliest on the face of this Earth, never shy to welcome visitors, always ready with a smile. Despite the difficult conditions that many Filipinos live under, there seems to be an almost universally positive outlook on life, something that even some Filipinos – let alone foreigners – find difficult to fathom. They certainly have a great capacity to live in and enjoy the moment, without worrying about what the future will bring. It is undoubtedly true that the strength of their extended families contributes hugely to a sense of personal security and belonging.

Below: The Philippines is a densely populated country, making the cities' streets often rather crowded, though almost always colourful and lively.

They also know how to party. Celebrations of all kinds figure large in Filipino life, providing regular opportunities to break off from the hard graft of daily toil. Every community, from the largest city to the smallest village, or *barangay*, has at least one annual fiesta to celebrate perhaps the harvest, an important historical event or a local patron saint,

providing regular opportunities for everyone to let their hair down. Some fiestas have become huge events with nationwide fame, the most important including Ati-Atihan in Kalibo, Dinagyang in Iloilo and Sinulog in Cebu City.

Unlike many Asian countries, women figure large in the Philippines' public life, taking on a wide range of prominent roles from managing small family-run businesses up to positions in local and national government. It is no coincidence that the Philippines has had two female presidents in the past 25 years, Corazon Aquino and Gloria Macapagal-Arroyo. The origin of this female equality is rather unclear, but there is evidence that it is buried deep in Philippine history, reaching back to matriarchal practices predating the 16th-century arrival of the Spanish.

Above: Filipino teenagers are like teenagers everywhere, wanting to be cool and fashionable. Here some are seen hanging out at a beachside cafe in Miagao, near Iloilo.

Left: Vast numbers of vibrant, colourful festivals are held across the country, one of the most famous being Iloilo's Dinagyang Festival, held each January.

Above: Festival musicians, complete with homemade drums, take a moment to relax between performances.

It is generally believed that most Filipinos are descended mainly from Austronesian peoples who arrived about 5,000 years ago from their homelands in Taiwan and/or southern China. Over this settlement has been laid a more modern input from Malay peoples (who also originated from the same Austronesians) arriving from the Indonesian islands on a number of occasions over the past 1,000 years. Those human migrations have created a patchwork of ethnic and cultural diversity, with about 90 per cent of Filipinos conforming to the mixed Austronesian-Malay description, often known locally as Pinoy. The remaining 10 per cent consist of quite a mixture of peoples ranging from those who are much more strongly Malay, generally living in the far south, to those with little or no Malay ancestry and so boasting almost pure Austronesian heritage. These people live mainly in the north, either in remote islands such as Batanes, or high in northern Luzon's Sierra Madre and Cordillera Central mountain ranges.

The plethora of cultural minority groups include such peoples as the Ifugao and Igorot in Luzon's mountains, the Ivatan in the Batanes Islands, or the T'boli, Badjao, Manobo and Yakan living in Mindanao and the Sulu Islands of the far south. In addition to all these groups there is one more, known by a variety of names, most commonly Negrito, Aeta, Ati or Agta. Often considered the Philippines' aboriginals, the Aeta too are thought to be immigrants, though ones who arrived about 20,000 years ago. Still living a largely hunter-gatherer existence in the country's forests, their numbers are in decline, at least in part due to the shrinking forest environment that sustains their lifestyle.

Below: The Ifugao are one of the most well known of the Philippines' minorities, living in northern Luzon's mountains, particularly around the town of Banaue. These days they rarely wear traditional clothing, seen here, generally reserving it for festivals and certain tourist locations.

Above: A Tagbanua fisherman, with one of his granddaughters, sits mending his fishing net in the village of Cabugao, on Coron Island, Palawan.

Above: An Aeta man seen building a bamboo lattice wall at a forest village near Subic Bay, northern Luzon.

Right: A Mangyan man cutting open a coconut, in the forests of Mount Malasimbo, near Puerto Galera, northern Mindoro.

Evidence of this cultural and ethnic diversity is found in the huge range of languages spoken across the country – estimated to be as many as 100. Most are used by the cultural minority groups, with just eight languages shared across the main Filipino population. Of these, two dominate: Tagalog and Cebuano, the former the language of northwestern Luzon, particularly around Manila, and the latter prevalent across the Visayas. English has been grafted onto this as a *lingua franca*. It is always surprising that, after 350 years of rule by Spain, the Spanish language is not more widespread. In fact, fragments of it are frequently heard in two main ways: firstly as words and expressions that have become integrated into the Filipino languages and secondly as names, both of places and of people.

The way in which foreign influences are readily absorbed by Philippine culture is one of the country's great wonders. It seems that few are ever completely rejected; most are absorbed, spun around a few times, slotted in among all the other customs and then expressed in daily life with a uniquely Filipino slant. Perhaps the most dramatic is the fervent devotion of the Filipino population to Catholicism. One of only two Christian countries in Asia (the other is East Timor), over 80 per cent of the population is Catholic, most regularly attending mass, with about another 10 per cent adhering to other Christian denominations. Not surprisingly, Catholicism has left a very visible mark upon the landscape in the form of now quite ancient and historic Spanish churches, fortress-like buildings dotted across the country. Most of the Philippines' festivals have a strongly Catholic slant, including processions devoted to local or national saints, particularly the Santo Niño (the infant Jesus), a very popular nationwide theme.

Left: The facade of Cebu Metropolitan Cathedral, dating from the 19th century, is typical of Spanish colonial architecture, marking both the dominance of Spain and Catholicism in the Philippines.

Above: The interior of the Basilica Minore del Santo Niño (see also page 62): a church that is much more important to the Cebuano people than the newer Cebu Cathedral. The 18th-century basilica houses a statue of Christ as a child, brought to the Philippines by Ferdinand Magellan.

Above: Residents of remote islands in the Siargao Island group (off northeast Mindanao) demonstrate their religious devotion by bringing their icons to be blessed at the cathedral in General Luna, Siargao's main town.

Left: Even the most riotous festival usually has a serious religious element, often the presentation of Santo Niño statues, as seen here at Dinagyang Festival, in Iloilo.

About half of the remaining 10 per cent of the population is Muslim, living mostly in the south of Mindanao and Palawan, as well as in the Sulu Islands. Almost all of these Muslims belong to one or another of the region's cultural minority groups, though far from all of the minorities here are Muslim. Known collectively as Lumad, the Mindanao-based non-Muslim cultural minorities are either Christian or animist in their beliefs. This is also true for most of the cultural minorities living across other parts of the Philippines.

History

There was a time when many accounts of Philippine history began in 1521, the year in which the Spanish first arrived under the command of Portuguese adventurer Ferdinand Magellan. Needless to say, however, the indigenous Filipino people had been living here for quite some time before the Europeans showed up and in the years since independence there has been a steady piecing together of what life was like in the pre-Hispanic centuries.

Although the earliest records of human settlement go back about 50,000 years to remains found in caves in southern Palawan, the main influx of people into the islands of the Philippines occurred about 5,000 years ago, when Austronesians migrated from southern China and/or Taiwan southwards through the archipelago.

Below: Remnants of the pre-Hispanic tradition of living in scattered rural communities, or 'barangay', rather than towns, can still be seen in the mountains of northern Luzon.

Above: A statue in Metro Manila's Makati district to Sultan Kudarat celebrates the 17th-century Islamic leader who resisted the Spanish invasion of southern Mindanao. Today, one of Mindanao's provinces is named after him.

For many centuries the Philippine islands existed with no single central authority, much of the population living in scattered autonomous communities, or *barangay*. Major trade centres grew up on the coasts, linked to (and often under the control of) one or another of the successive Indianized empires that came and went along the coasts of Southeast Asia.

Chinese records show that the most important of these trade centres became Cebu, Butuan and Tondo, the last of these very close to the site of modern Manila's port, while the other two remain as important cities. Chinese ships – which dominated the seas of Southeast Asia at this time – began trading with these ports at least as early as the 9th century.

From the 13th century onwards, Muslim missionaries began arriving in the southernmost Philippine islands. Islam

Above: *The Magellan Cross, set against a frescoed ceiling, marks the spot in Cebu City where Ferdinand Magellan planted the original cross in 1521, starting the Christianization of the Philippines.*

steadily spread northwards, the first Philippine Islamic sultanate being established in southern Mindanao in the 15th century.

Ferdinand Magellan arrived in Cebu with three ships in April 1521, having crossed the Pacific in search of an east–west route to the Spice Islands, in today's Indonesia. He quickly set about converting the local chief, Humabon, his wife and his followers to Christianity but came unstuck when he ran up against Lapu-Lapu, chief of nearby Mactan Island. In the ensuing battle, Magellan was killed, and the rest of his crew were lucky to escape with their lives. Today, Lapu-Lapu is hailed as the Philippines' first national hero.

For several decades the Spanish made little serious attempt to control the Philippines, but all that changed when Miguel López de Legazpi arrived in 1565. He took over Cebu and built Fort San Pedro – still seen today – before moving his base to a more easily defended site at today's Iloilo, on the island of Panay. He then captured both Tondo and nearby Maynilad, the two together forming the nucleus for Manila, centred on the mouth of the Pasig River.

Spanish control of the Philippines lasted for 350 years, until the end of the 19th century when mounting resistance, led by such national heroes as José Rizal and Emilio Aguinaldo, led to Spain's departure. Unfortunately, it was replaced by a new colonial power, the United States. By the 1930s, however, plans were in place to grant independence, though this suffered a blow with the Japanese attack on Pearl Harbor in Hawaii in 1941, followed quickly by their invasion of the Philippines. By the end of 1944, however,

Above: A statue in Cebu City of Miguel López de Legazpi, founder of the first permanent Spanish settlement in the Philippines.

Below: The internal compound of Fort San Pedro, in Cebu City; the first permanent Spanish building in the Philippines, built in 1565.

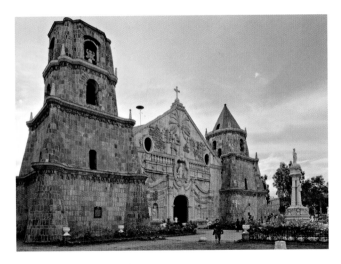

the Americans were back, with General Douglas MacArthur at the head of a massive military force.

The Philippines finally gained independence in 1946, since which the country has been a democratic republic run by a US-style Congress headed by a powerful president. There has been one major hiatus in this period – that of the dictatorship of Ferdinand Marcos. Elected in 1965, by 1972 he had declared martial law, holding onto power until 1986 when he was finally forced to flee by a mass uprising, the People Power Revolution.

Since then, successive governments have struggled to rebuild the shattered economy, and though quite successful, they have been dogged by endemic corruption. Periodic communist and Islamic insurgencies, mostly in the far south, took their toll too, especially in the 1980s when unrest became almost nationwide. Improving economic conditions, coupled with a series of treaties, including the creation of a Muslim autonomous region in Mindanao, had greatly reduced the feeling of national discontent by the late 1990s. In recent years, however, there has been a modest resurgence, mainly from Islamists and the communist New People's Army in remote areas of the far south. Despite this, the great majority of the country is essentially peaceful and economically has managed to ride out the global recession reasonably well.

Above left: Miagao Church near Iloilo (see also page 50) is now a World Heritage Site due to its spectacular facade.

Above: The entrance into one of the heavily fortified bastions in the old walls surrounding Intramuros, the original Spanish capital, in Manila.

Above: The Rizal Monument, in Manila's Rizal Park, memorializes José Rizal, father of the Philippine nation, executed near here in 1896.

The Economy

Though the Philippine economy has been growing strongly in recent times, it remains one of the weaker Southeast Asian nations, a continuing legacy of the damage done during the corrupt Marcos years. Wealth distribution is extremely uneven, the richest few per cent of the population controlling much of the economy, the poorest taking on average earnings of about US$40 per month.

Industrialization programmes have had an impact in some areas but most factories remain concentrated around Manila and Cebu. Mining is of major importance to the national economy; rich deposits of copper, gold, silver, manganese and nickel bringing in valuable foreign currency. Unfortunately the mines employ relatively few people. Services, including government and tourism, provide work for over half the population, though again they are predominantly focused on the main cities.

Top: The rice harvest, happening at different times across the country, includes spreading the grains out to dry before storing.

Above: Manila's container port, seen at dusk, is one of the Philippines' main trade connections to the outside world.

Left: Across many rural areas rice farming is king, particularly in the steep terraced fields of mountainous northern Luzon.

Right: Fishing, practised mainly as a subsistence activity, is crucial to many poor coastal communities, and is carried out mainly inshore and using small outrigger boats equipped with small-meshed nets.

Below: Quiapo Market, in the northern part of Manila, is a crowded and often frenetic scene of small-scale family-driven enterprise, with everything from mangoes to fortune-telling for sale.

Agriculture and fishing remain overwhelmingly the main rural employment, shaping much of the inland and coastal landscape. These are probably the aspects of the Philippine economy that are most visible to the visitor. Not surprisingly, rice predominates; more than four million hectares (about 10 million acres) are devoted to the crop. Through the year alternating waves of emerald green or golden yellow billow across the landscape.

A similar amount of land is covered with coconut palms, an estimated 220 million of them covering coast and countryside with their characteristic green canopy. Their output makes the Philippines one of the world's biggest producers of coconut products. Other important crops include sugar cane, coffee and pineapples, grown mostly on large commercial scale plantations.

It remains a fact of life, however, that there just isn't enough work available, a situation made worse by the rapidly growing population. Its present level of almost 100 million is increasing by nearly 2 per cent annually. As a result, the last 25 years have seen a growing flood of Filipinos travelling abroad to work. Millions are now employed crewing ships, putting up buildings, nursing the sick and elderly and acting as domestic helps right around the globe. Their financial remittances from abroad have become essential to help support families left at home and they have become a major sector of the national economy, their financial contribution amounting now to a staggering US$11 billion annually.

Visiting the Islands

With its many stunning white coral sand beaches, the coast is undoubtedly the country's main draw, most especially in the Visayas and Palawan regions. The pre-eminent attraction is Boracay, a tiny island barely eight km (five miles) long, the appropriately named White Beach running more than half its length. Other well known beach resorts include Panglao Island, El Nido, Puerto Galera and San Fernando. Some of these are now becoming popular tourist destinations, but many stretches of untouched golden sand remain, beckoning the adventurous, particularly in the remoter parts of Palawan, and on some of the smaller islands off the coasts of Cebu and Mindanao.

The mountainous interior has been largely overlooked by tourism, with the exception of the Cordillera Central mountains of northern Luzon. Here the magnificent mountainside rice terraces, a World Heritage Site around the village of Banaue that were first constructed around 2,000 years ago, are the main attraction. Those in search of cooler weather head for the heights of Baguio; at some 1,500 m (5,000 ft) above sea level it is the Philippines' only high-altitude city.

Opposite above: In recent years accommodation in many resorts has headed upmarket, as illustrated by this dusk view of Discovery Shores, one of Boracay's most exclusive resorts.

Below: Outrigger boats, or 'bancas', as seen here in El Nido, Palawan, are widely used for inter-island travel and almost universal in local water-borne tours.

Below: The Philippines' number one attraction is undoubtedly Boracay Island, due almost entirely to its spectacular White Beach, several kilometres of white sand stretching along much of the island's west coast.

Wildlife watching is still in its infancy in the Philippines, partly as a result of the rather secretive forest-bound nature of many of the animals that live there. However, whale- and dolphin-watching, as well as bird-watching, are increasingly well organized. Bird-watching trips to a variety of forests around the country are now quite common, particularly Subic Bay, Mount Makiling and St Paul's Underground River. Whale- and dolphin-watching are largely a preserve of the Visayas, most particularly off the southern coast of Bohol and in the Tanon Straits between Negros and Cebu. Close to the southern Luzon town of Donsol for several months of the year it is possible to spot and go swimming with Whale Sharks, which congregate there in large numbers.

Adventure Sports

For many years virtually the only well developed adventure sport for visitors was diving, but recently other leisure activities have started to be offered, including, surfing, kite-boarding, hiking, mountain biking, sea angling and white water rafting.

The Philippines has some of the best dive sites in Asia, its protected reefs a magnificently chaotic jumble of corals, home to a wonderful diversity of brilliantly colourful fish. Every beach resort has well organized dive operations, offering plenty of diving opportunities, including globally recognized training and qualification courses.

Still on the water, windsurfing and kite-surfing have started to take off, particularly along Bulabog Beach on the east shore of Boracay. At its best during the onshore winds of the northeast monsoon (blowing approximately from November to March), Bulabog has become a major venue for international competitions.

Below: Kite-surfers prepare for a day's action at Bulabog Beach, on the east shore of Boracay Island, the Philippines' premier windsurfing and kite-surfing venue.

Above: A mountain guide stands on the summit of Mount Apo, the Philippines' highest mountain, after leading hikers up from Lake Agco at the roadhead.

Further south, the Siargao Islands, off the northeast coast of Mindanao and exposed to the full swell of the Pacific Ocean, have become known as the Philippines' premier surfing hotspot. Discovered in the 1990s by Australian surfing 'scouts', Siargao is particularly renowned for the so-called Cloud Nine surf break. Sea angling is also growing in popularity here, taking advantage of the area's deep Pacific waters.

Mountain hiking is increasingly available and although it is possible to arrange your own hikes (always take a guide), specialist operators also regularly organize hikes up several of the country's volcanoes, including Mount Apo, the Philippines' highest peak.

Two of the great bonuses of doing anything in the Philippines are firstly the fact that the vast majority of the population speak good English, and secondly that Filipinos are almost without exception wonderfully friendly, helpful and hospitable to visitors, making getting around both a joy and relatively easy. All visitors need are a little patience, a sense of humour and the enthusiasm to get stuck in and enjoy themselves!

Above: *A boatman steers his 'banca' away from White Island, an increasingly popular sandy island off Camiguin Island, Mindanao.*

Right: *A diver rises up a submarine cliff towards the surface, at Tubbataha Reef, off the coast of Palawan.*

Chapter 2: The North

The north of the Philippines takes in most of Luzon, the Philippines' largest island, plus the island of Mindoro, nestling against Luzon's southwest coast. It is a hugely diverse region, ranging from Manila, the national capital and by far the largest metropolis, to some of the country's wildest and remotest terrain, complete with high mountains and dense rainforest. In both city and countryside lie a range of visitor attractions, particularly parts of Manila, the massive rice terraces of Banaue and the beaches and coral reefs of Puerto Galera.

Below: A view at dusk along Roxas Boulevard of the Ermita and Malate districts of Manila. These downtown centres have much of the city's tourism infrastructure, being filled with hotels and restaurants.

Manila

This massive metropolis of over 16 million inhabitants is the Philippines' economic and political heart. The main visitor attraction is Intramuros, the old Spanish city that was the focus of the colonial government, surrounded by massive stone walls. Sadly, few of the original buildings remain due to heavy damage inflicted during the Second World War,

Left: With shops and restaurants lining a meandering stretch of water, softened and shaded by palms, trees, orchids and a host of other plants, the upmarket Greenbelt Plaza is a rare green urban oasis, a feature of Metro Manila's Makati district.

but at its heart stands Manila Cathedral, rebuilt after the war on the same site occupied by several predecessors down the centuries. To the south of Intramuros lies Rizal Park, a large open green space, and the site of the execution in 1896 of national hero José Rizal. Beyond stretches a seashore promenade along Roxas Boulevard, southwards to the yacht marina.

To get two very different tastes of commercial Manila, first head north of the Pasig River to the Quiapo district; the area's narrow streets are crammed with markets and perpetually jammed with shoppers. From here, cross over to Makati for a taste of the modern city with its gleaming skyscrapers, upmarket boutiques and air-conditioned malls, a whole world away from the more traditional Asia north of the river.

Right: The central nave of Manila Cathedral, centre of Catholicism in the Philippines. Destroyed several times down the centuries, today's cathedral dates only from the 1950s.

Above: The lobby bar of the Pan Pacific Hotel is typical of the modern chic design that has swept through Manila's top-class hotels in recent years.

Left: The crowded, bustling streets of Quiapo are typical of the old parts of Manila lying north of the Pasig River. Here are many of the city's poorer districts, some of the most densely populated places on Earth.

Left: A mobile 'snack shop' pedals along the seafront promenade on Roxas Boulevard just before sunset. In recent years this seafront area has become a popular place to relax in the cooler hours of sunset and dusk.

Below: One of the best places in Manila to pick up a wide range of fruit is the San Andres Market in Malate, where everything from apples to rambutan can be found.

Above: Fruit and dried fish piled up on stalls in Quiapo Market typify the everyday produce available to the crowds of shoppers here.

The Rice Terraces of Banaue

This World Heritage Site on the southern edge of Luzon's Cordillera Central mountains is home to a network of 2,000-year-old terraced rice fields that climb steeply up the mountainsides. Irrigated by a complex system of water channels, most of the terraces are still farmed by the Ifugao people, descendants of the terraces' ancient builders. These terraces offer the visitor an often vibrantly green and always intensely rural scene.

The central hub of the region is the small town of Banaue, where most accommodation is located, but the best rice terraces are found in remoter valleys around the villages of Hapao and Batad. The latter are undoubtedly the most spectacular, clinging to the steep sides of an amphitheatre-like valley, but they are reachable only on foot.

These pages: The steeply terraced rice fields in the countryside around Banaue are really the central feature for visitors to this region. When the rice plants are young, the terraces are a swathe of stunningly vibrant emerald green. In some areas the terraces are sculpted across a relatively gentle landscape, interspersed with clusters of betel nut palms, source of a mild drug that the local people chew, such as around Hapao (below). At a higher altitude, the steep terrain requires some spectacularly deep and complex terraces, most especially around the village of Batad (right and below left). Roads connecting most villages are narrow, steep and twisting, and the only form of public transport is the ubiquitous jeepney (left), services regularly linking the villages to Banaue.

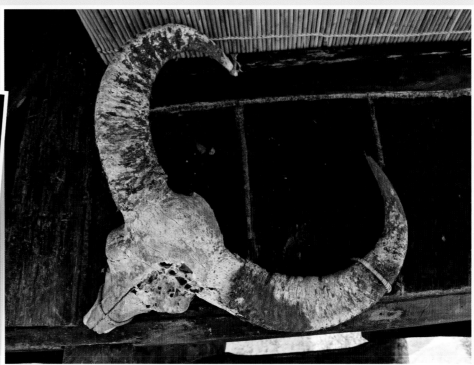

These pages: The Ifugao people, one of the Philippines' most well known cultural minorities, were the original builders of Banaue's rice terraces about 2,000 years ago. Today, they still farm many of the terraces. Their traditional clothing consists largely of red woven cloth, though it is rarely seen these days. Headgear is frequently decorated with feathers (below right), with the most elaborate featuring hornbill casques (right), while other adornments might include pendants made from animal bones (below). Their wooden homes are usually built on stilts, and while these are still common, the traditional thatch roof is being increasingly replaced by sheet metal. Some thatched houses have been preserved, such as those at the outdoor museum at Hawang (left). Houses are still commonly adorned with the paraphernalia of rural life, including portable chicken coops (below far left) and water buffalo skulls (below left).

Puerto Galera

One of the best known beach resort areas in the Philippines, Puerto Galera lies on and around a peninsula near the northern tip of Mindoro. It is centred on the village of Muelle, which sits on a stunningly beautiful natural harbour formed by a series of drowned valleys. This used to be an important anchorage for Spanish galleons, hence the name. To both east and west lie a string of small bays, each home to a village and collection of resorts, the largest being Sabang, east of Muelle. The most beautiful beaches are west of Muelle, at White Beach and Aninuan, but Puerto Galera's main attraction is diving, well-protected coral reefs offering a string of stunning and easily accessible dive sites.

Top: With few roads in and around Puerto Galera, 'bancas' represent the best way to get around. As a result, many of the beaches are lined with them, as seen here at a village in the entrance to the Muelle harbour.

Above: Puerto Galera's well-protected reefs and well-established diving operations attract scuba divers from all over the world. Here a group of Japanese divers makes its way across a reef flat.

Above: A group of divers comes ashore at Sabang after an early morning dive. With almost all the reefs easily accessible via a short boat trip across well-sheltered waters, most dives need use only small, lightweight boats.

Left: A dive group prepares to head out from Big La Laguna Beach, using a traditional 'banca' to reach the reef. With so many divers visiting Puerto Galera, dive groups come and go from the various resorts all day, every day.

Above: In early morning sunlight, 'bancas' at Small La Laguna Beach are readied for the day's tours and diving trips.

Left: At dusk, a coconut palm leaning across Small La Laguna Beach becomes a glowing advert for a beachside restaurant.

Opposite: The beautiful golden light of sunset illuminates coconut palms, shops and cafés along the waterfront at Sabang. Here the buildings crowd so close to the shore that at high tide no beach remains to be seen.

Above: One of the longest-established hotels on Big La Laguna Beach is La Laguna Beach Club and Resort. It is an important dive centre and a mecca for divers.

Left: A cluster of corals, the most prominent of which is the large Mushroom Leather Coral, 'Sarcophyton' species, on one of the reefs of Puerto Galera.

Right: At Big La Laguna Beach, actually quite a small beach, lines of 'bancas' crowd the seashore, while clusters of lodges and hotels line the beach, providing all the facilities that visitors to Puerto Galera could need.

Above: One of Puerto Galera's boatmen helms his 'banca', a water taxi linking the beaches and resorts, through the narrow channel that separates Muelle harbour from the sea.

Chapter 3: Central Philippines

Taking in the northern part of the Visayas and Palawan, this is a sprawling area of scattered islands, many of them home to stunning white beaches and offshore coral reefs, including Boracay and El Nido, two of the country's most popular resort areas. The region also hosts some spectacular annual festivals, most notably Dinagyang held each January in the city of Iloilo.

Iloilo is both one of the Visayas' most important cities and a historic place, a site colonized by the Spanish in the very early days of their takeover of the Philippines. The surrounding area bears some of the marks of the colonial presence, mainly in the form of fortress-like churches, the most famous being a World Heritage Site, located in the town of Miagao.

Boracay

The Philippines' most popular tourist attraction, Boracay is a tiny island, barely eight km (five miles) long, lying off the northern tip of Panay, one of the Visayas' main landmasses. Discovered as a holiday paradise in the 1980s by backpacking travellers, the draw has always been its incredible White Beach that stretches five km (three miles) along the west coast. While those early backpackers might have found only very basic accommodation, today Boracay boasts some world-class resort hotels and is very much a mainstream tourism destination. Though it might be difficult to find solitude on White Beach these days, the sand remains stunningly white and fine, and the sea azure and crystal clear.

Right: An afternoon view of the northern end of Boracay's magnificent White Beach. Stretching along much of the island's west coast, White Beach is lined for almost its whole length with restaurants, bars, hotels and the ubiquitous coconut palm.

Left: A sailing outrigger, or 'paraw', sits on the shore at the southern end of White Beach awaiting customers. 'Paraws' are widely available for hire on Boracay, for peaceful wind-driven tours around the island, free from the typical clatter of a 'banca' engine!

Below: The northern end of White Beach, Boracay. Sun-loungers, parasols, swaying coconut palms, fine white coral sand and a gently lapping azure sea; what more could one ask for from the archetypal tropical beach retreat?

Left: At Puka Beach, close to Boracay's northern tip, a souvenir stall displays wind chimes made from shaped and painted sea shells.

Below: Along much of its length, White Beach is backed by a sandy traffic-free path, lined by hundreds of shops, restaurants, bars and hotels, plus a liberal scattering of souvenir and snack stalls, all catering to a wide-ranging international clientele.

Above left: A dusk view of one of Boracay's most long-established hotels, the wood- and bamboo-clad Fridays, situated close to the northern end of White Beach, well-removed from the bustle of the main developments further south.

Above right: The beach bar at one of White Beach's most modern and exclusive hotels, Discovery Shores. Lying near the beach's northern end, it is an upmarket vision of white concrete and glass, climbing the hill behind the beach.

Left: Built of thatch and coconut timber, Nigi Nigi Nu Noos is a long-established restaurant in the centre of White Beach. These traditional materials were standard on Boracay a few years ago, ensuring that development blended in well with the rural setting, though this is increasingly giving way to concrete.

Left: A view southwards along the length of White Beach, showing just how busy the beach is, with crowds of bathers and clusters of 'paraws', or sailing outriggers. The abundance of the vegetation behind the beach is also clear while in the distance a thunderstorm gathers over the mountains of mainland Panay.

Below: At low tide a stack of coralline rock sits in a shallow pool at the northernmost end of White Beach. Though mostly sandy, the beach's shore does have the occasional coral rock outcrop, the remnants of long-lost ancient reefs.

Right: At a particularly popular part of White Beach, near its southern end, towering coconut palms lean over the beach, providing an exotic backdrop for bathers.

Iloilo and its Surroundings

Iloilo may not initially appear to be the most obvious of places to visit, but it is nevertheless worth exploring for a number of reasons. Each January Iloilo hosts what is undoubtedly one of the Philippines' most spectacular festivals, Dinagyang, during which the city's streets are filled with dance troupes competing in hugely colourful and elaborately choreographed performances.

Outside festival season, the surrounding area is worth exploring for its string of historic Spanish-era churches, most especially that at Miagao, a World Heritage Site that is protected for its wonderful façade.

For those who like wandering on beaches, although long stretches of golden sand and turquoise water are hard to find, here these are replaced by busy, friendly, fishing communities, where you can watch the catch being brought ashore, along with boats being repaired, launched and returned.

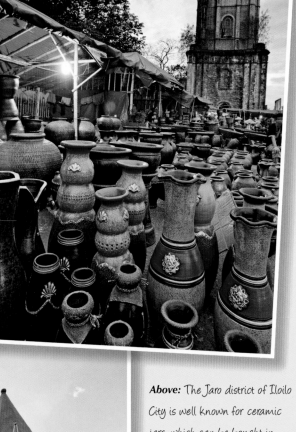

Above: The Jaro district of Iloilo City is well known for ceramic jars, which can be bought in Belfry Plaza, dominated by the Spanish-era Belfry, as shown in this dusk shot.

Left: Miagao Church is one of the Philippines' most famous man-made landmarks. Built between 1787 and 1797, it is a World Heritage Site due to its stunning exterior depicting St Christopher in a tropical garden.

Above: Having just returned from a fishing trip and pulled their boat up onto the beach at Miagao, fishermen sort through the catch in preparation for selling it to friends and neighbours gathering around.

Left: The Iloilo area is renowned in the Philippines for its high quality weaving, including cloth produced on the handlooms of Indag-an Cooperative in Miagao, shown here.

These pages: In a country renowned for its festivals, Iloilo's Dinagyang is arguably one of the Philippines' most spectacular. Held annually over the third weekend of January, events kick off on the Friday evening with a huge food festival, hundreds of food stalls setting up on the streets. One of the most popular dishes is grilled satay (far right). The Saturday is dominated by the Kasadyahan dance competition, taking place in several grandstands set up on Iloilo's streets. Amateur dance groups from local colleges and villages get to strut their stuff, with huge, lavishly choreographed performances that aim to celebrate such aspects of local life as fishing (above and right) or agriculture (left). Outside the grandstands, the crowded streets are lined with stalls selling snacks and mementoes (above right).

These pages: The main event of Dinagyang Festival is Ati-Atihan, held on the Sunday. It commemorates land deals agreed between the native Aeta tribes and Malays immigrating from Borneo in the 12th and 13th centuries, allowing the Malays to settle in Panay. Consisting of a dance competition held in grandstands set up on Iloilo's streets, enormous amateur dance groups stage stunningly elaborate performances, complete with blackened skin and hugely spectacular tribal-style costumes that aim to recall the beneficent Aeta tribes.

El Nido

A remote location on Palawan's northern coast, El Nido is arguably one of the Philippines' most beautiful areas. Named after the town that is the area's one and only hub, El Nido consists of an archipelago of small islands scattered across sheltered Bacuit Bay. The bay's landscape is formed largely of almost sheer karst limestone cliffs similar to those seen in the wonderful mountain peaks of southwest China or southern Thailand, some plunging hundreds of metres straight into the sea. Among these cliffs are scattered occasional golden sandy beaches, each usually backed by a small cluster of coconut palms and reachable only by boat. It is hard to imagine anywhere better for those wanting to really escape the rat race and play at being Robinson Crusoe for a while!

Above: The coast around El Nido is characterized by enormous limestone cliffs, the less steep parts covered with dense rainforests.

Below left: This particularly spectacular karst limestone pinnacle and cliff stands guard over the approach to Lagen Island, one of many rocky islands in El Nido's Bacuit Bay.

Above: At dusk the stunning outlines of the limestone rocks and cliffs in Bacuit Bay, as seen here on Lagen Island, become really apparent, while the soft colours give a sense of calm and peace.

Left: One of the great attractions of beautiful Bacuit Bay is the number of beaches that lie in many of the small coves, almost all accessible only by boat. Shown here is Seven Commandoes Beach, quite close to El Nido town.

Above: *A street scene in El Nido town, with motor tricycles, the local taxis, and signs in Spanish (the guesthouse), English (American names on the tricycles), and native Pilipino (advertising in the shop).*

Left: *On El Nido town's central plaza, a pleasant open space outside local government buildings, motor tricycles wait for passengers in the shade of a stunningly beautiful tree.*

Above: Using a bamboo pole to manoeuvre a 'banca' away from a beach in Bacuit Bay. The engines of many Philippine 'bancas' have no reverse gear, so backing away from the shore can be a tricky process.

Left: El Nido's harbour consists of a huge, natural harbour surrounded by high cliffs and forested hills. Hundreds of boats sit on moorings, using the beach as their passenger and cargo pick-up and drop-off area.

Right: The bar and restaurant area of the exclusive Lagen Island Resort sits right beside the shore in a sheltered cove on Lagen Island, deep in Bacuit Bay.

Below: A dusk view of the beautiful Lagen Island Resort, showing some of its bungalows, standing on stilts in the shallows of a protected cove, and backed by sheer limestone cliffs.

Above: Most visitors coming to stay at Lagen Island and Miniloc Island Resorts, arrive by air. The resorts have their own jeepney that shuttles their guests from the airport to the harbour for the boat ride out to the islands.

Right: Coconut palms stand clear of rainforest and backed by sheer cliffs on Lagen Island. While many of Bacuit Bay's islands are forested, on Lagen Island the presence of a resort has greatly improved that island's forest protection.

Chapter 4: The South

Comprising the southernmost Visayan islands, Mindanao and Sulu, the places in the south that are of most interest to visitors lie in the northern part of this region. The main hub is Cebu City, the country's second most important urban area and a major centre of international trade for many hundreds of years. To the south lies the intensely rural Bohol, home of rice fields, the Chocolate Hills and some of the Philippines' best beaches and coral reefs. Further south still lies the vast mountainous expanse of Mindanao, relatively infrequently visited by tourists and offering the curious a beautiful and wonderfully laid-back taster in the form of Camiguin Island, lying just off Mindanao's north coast.

Cebu

The south's economic powerhouse, Cebu City is the most important city, economically speaking, in the region and capital of Cebu Province, a long pencil-thin island running north to south in the southern Visayas. The urban area falls neatly into old and new parts, with most places of visitor interest lying in the former, primarily relics dating from the period of Spanish rule. To the city's east lies Mactan Island, site of Cebu's international airport and a string of resort hotels lined up along the island's south coast. A significant proportion of Mactan's population is involved in making guitars, a long-established traditional industry on the island. These are not cheap toys or souvenirs produced for the tourist industry, but beautifully made classical and Spanish-style acoustic instruments crafted in a host of different models and wood types for a discerning clientele.

Right: The Basilica Minore del Santo Niño is one of the Philippines' most important churches, home to the infant Jesus statue brought to the country by Ferdinand Magellan in the 16th century.

Above: The compound of Fort San Pedro. Built in 1565, this was the first permanent Spanish building to be erected in the Philippines.

Below: A pile of vegetables at a stall in Carbon Market, a bustling agricultural produce market lining a network of streets in the old part of Cebu City. This is a vital sales point for farm produce coming in from across Cebu island.

Above: A small flower market adorns a side street in the old part of Cebu City, opposite the Basilica Minore del Santo Niño.

Above: The owner of a guitar factory on Mactan Island finishes tuning a new guitar. A long-established industry on Mactan, guitar-making is still a major industry, employing a large proportion of the island's population.

Left: Wholly made by hand, Mactan's guitars are not cheap souvenirs, but beautifully crafted musical instruments, made by skilled workers, produced using woods brought in from around the world.

Above: A dusk view of one of the poolside lodges at Plantation Bay Resort, on Mactan Island. Due to the proximity of the international airport, Mactan's tourism consists of largely upmarket hotels and resorts.

Right: A poolside pavilion at Mactan's Plantation Bay Resort offers the perfect opportunity to simply relax in the shade and enjoy the view.

Bohol

A largely rural island southeast of Cebu, most visitors head straight for Panglao, a small island close to Bohol's southwest coast. Beautiful white sandy beaches stretch along Panglao's south coast, the most well known and busiest being Alona Beach. A major attraction is diving, particularly around nearby Balicasag Island, a marine reserve renowned for its sheer submarine cliffs and large shoals of colourful fish.

The main island of Bohol is deservedly being more and more widely explored. For years, the main attraction has been the weirdly shaped Chocolate Hills, a landscape of large rounded 'humps' near Bohol's centre. However, increasingly visitors are looking further afield, such as at the island's numerous Spanish-era churches, its waterfalls and the tarsier sanctuary, a centre for breeding this threatened tiny primate unique to the forests of the south.

These pages: Alona Beach is the main visitor attraction on Panglao Island, its long sandy shore lined with both coconut palms and restaurants. In the evening, tables are laid out on the sands to allow for 'al fresco' waterside dining under the palms (above). The menu includes a wide range of locally caught and extremely fresh seafood from snapper to octopus (right). As at many beaches, 'bancas' line the shore in the early morning, ready for the day's diving and whale-watching trips, as well as sightseeing tours around the coastline (left). Diving is a major sport here. Not only are there several good dive sites around Panglao's coast but also, more importantly, a little offshore lies Balicasag Island, a marine sanctuary renowned for its spectacular coral and fish life. It's a common sight every morning to see diving equipment piled up on the beach ready for the day's first dives (above left).

Above: Divers ascend towards the surface, climbing the near-vertical submarine wall that surrounds Balicasag Island. A well-protected marine sanctuary, Balicasag is a major draw for divers, who use Alona Beach as the most convenient base.

Right: A close-up detail of a 'Dendronephthya' species soft tree coral, growing on the submarine wall off Balicasag Island. Tree corals are beautiful and colourful structures, rarely more than about 15 cm (6 in) tall but always totally eye-catching.

Opposite: A calm dusk view at ChARTS Resort, a lovely example of the many small, independently run hotels and resorts that typify Alona Beach.

Above: *Along Bohol's south coast, a little east of Panglao Island, is the 17th-century Baclayon Church, believed to be one of the earliest Spanish churches built in the Philippines.*

Left: *Lying in central Bohol, the weirdly shaped Chocolate Hills – so named for their brown colour at the end of the dry season – are one of the Philippines' icons and arguably Bohol's main visitor attraction.*

Above: Nipa palms in a mangrove swamp on Bohol's southwest coast. Nipa is used extensively for roof thatch and so is often actively cultivated in Bohol's many mangroves.

Above: At barely 8 cm (3 in) long, excluding its tail, the Philippine Tarsier, 'Tarsius syrichta', is possibly the world's smallest primate. This one is at the Tarsier Sanctuary, a captive breeding centre near Corella.

Above: The lovely Mag-Aso Falls, one of Bohol's more accessible waterfalls, cascades through rainforest in the southwest of the island.

Camiguin

This spectacular jewel is another of the Philippines' most beautiful remote locations, a place to slip out of the rat race and just relax. In a country renowned globally for its relaxed friendliness, Camiguin is king, famous even among Filipinos for its unrivalled peace and serenity.

Volcanism dominates in the form of five massive volcanoes towering over the entire island, one of which – Hibok-Hibok – is active. The grey sand beaches that they have created ensure that this will never become another Boracay-type picture-postcard resort. What it does have, however – quite apart from superbly friendly locals – is a lush forest and farmland landscape, spectacular waterfalls, inviting hot springs and a curious white sand bar a little way offshore that offers a superb view back to the island.

These pages: Most of Camiguin's life goes on along its coastline and the narrow flat strip of land circling the island between shore and mountain. For visitors, the main attraction is White Island (left), a permanent white sand bar off Camiguin's north coast and something of a curiosity on this island of grey volcanic sand. For the locals, fishing is the main livelihood, the beaches and shoreside coconut groves filled with fishing boats (below, far left), ready to be launched at any time. Almost all the fishing is carried out inshore by small, family-run boats and is largely a subsistence livelihood. Hand-thrown nets are the main tool, the catch being cleaned out after returning to shore, as seen in this image of fishermen at work on the beach at Agoho on Camiguin's northern shore (below left). A multitude of multi-coloured floats are used to keep one edge of the net afloat (below right), while the rest sinks, creating a vertical wall in which to trap fish.

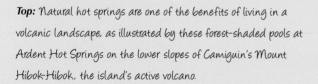

Top: Natural hot springs are one of the benefits of living in a volcanic landscape, as illustrated by these forest-shaded pools at Ardent Hot Springs on the lower slopes of Camiguin's Mount Hibok-Hibok, the island's active volcano.

Above: Many of Camiguin's rural people love to garden, so it is quite common to see homes adorned with a huge array of vibrantly colourful and fragrant flowers.

Above: Katibawasan Falls, Camiguin's most spectacular waterfall and a popular attraction for both visitors and locals, cascading down a cliff on the lower slopes of Mount Hibok-Hibok.

Left: Intensively farmed rice fields on the lower slopes of Mount Hibok-Hibok. The soil at the foot of the volcano is immensely fertile, making agriculture slightly risky but incredibly productive.

Above: Chilling out at a rural road junction, a motorcyclist and tricycle driver meet up to relax and pass the hottest part of the day by taking things easy.

Getting About

Simply moving around in the Philippines is one of its joys – a vast public transport network makes almost everywhere accessible. Your travel options run the full gamut from aircraft to spluttering motor boats and on to jeepneys (brightly decorated Jeep conversions), tricycles and motorbikes. Moreover, it is often quite a sociable experience, the crews almost universally friendly and helpful, ready to go to great lengths to help out.

Below: The passenger ferry route linking Puerto Galera to Luzon is run almost entirely by surprisingly large and powerful 'bancas', such as this one preparing to leave Puerto Galera's Muelle harbour.

Not surprisingly, the most convenient form of long-distance trans-island travel is the domestic airline network, operated mainly by Philippine Airlines although a growing number of other operators, such as Cebu Pacific Air and Southeast Asia Airlines, now contribute routes. However, island-hopping by boat is one of the great adventures of Philippine travel, making for an experience unique to the country. Although most of the mid-length routes are operated by sleek, fast, air-conditioned catamarans, most shorter routes are run by *bancas*, or pump-boats. These are traditional Philippine craft with long narrow hulls that are stabilized by huge outriggers usually made of multiple bamboo poles. Ideal for the sheltered shallow waters of the Philippine islands, air-conditioning comes in the form of the sea breeze coupled with the occasional shower of spray from the boat's outriggers. Keep your camera well-protected!

Left: The jeepney is without doubt the quintessentially Philippine mode of public transport. Brilliantly painted and decorated, immensely noisy and usually belching clouds of smoke, they are the backbone of the country's rural transport.

Below: For those cross-town hops, the tricycle is definitely the way to go. Whether carrying luggage-laden tourists or a gaggle of local schoolgirls, these little machines do their job superbly.

On land, long-distance routes across the larger islands, particularly Luzon and Mindanao, are covered by a plethora of buses from a host of competing companies. Comfort levels and prices vary enormously between companies but the best buses operating out of the main cities are usually very comfortable, to the point of being excessively air-conditioned – always be sure to take some warm clothing onto such a bus. Remoter rural areas – as well as many urban routes – are often served exclusively by that quintessentially Philippine form of transport, the jeepney. Cheap and practical, they are also very slow, crowded and – especially for tall people – painfully uncomfortable! They are, however, immensely sociable, allowing visitors truly to get in touch with rural Philippine life in a way that probably would not be possible otherwise.

Taxis are, of course, very handy for those cross-town hops, particularly when carrying luggage. However, they generally don't exist in small towns and out in the countryside, and are replaced instead by motorized tricycles – motorbikes with a covered and often vibrantly painted sidecar attached. In remote rural locations even these might not be an option, in which case taxis will usually come with

two wheels, in other words a ride on the back of a motorbike for a very modest fee. Be sure not to have too much luggage if you decide to take this option!

Resources

Below are listed a range of companies and organizations that you may find useful in planning a Philippines trip.

Tourism Information

Philippine Department of Tourism:
www.wowphilippines.co.uk
www.philippinetourism.com.au

Airlines

Cathay Pacific Airways: www.cathaypacific.com
Philippine Airlines: www.philippineairlines.com
Air Philippines (Philippine Airlines budget airline):
www.airphilexpress.com

Hotels

Manila: Manila Hotel; www.manila-hotel.com.ph
Pan Pacific Manila Hotel; www.panpacific.com
Oxford Suites Makati Hotel;
www.oxfordsuitesmakati.com
Banaue: Banaue Hotel and Youth Hostel;
www.philtourism.com/bhyh_desc.html
Boracay: Discovery Shores Boracay Island;
www.discoveryshoresboracay.com
Fridays Boracay; www.fridaysboracay.com
Iloilo: Century 21 Hotel; www.ann2.net/hotels/century21/
El Nido: Lagen Island Resort; www.elnidoresorts.com
Lally and Abet Beach Resort; www.lallyandabet.com
Cebu: Plantation Bay, Mactan Island;
www.plantationbay.com
Panglao Island, Bohol, Eskaya Resort;
www.eskayaresort.com
ChARTs Resort Alona Beach; www.charts-alona.com
Camiguin: Caves Dive Resort;
www.cavesdiveresortcamiguin.com

Further Reading

Bergbauer, M. and M. Kirschner. 2010. *Diving & Snorkelling Guide to Tropical Marine Life of the Indo-Pacific Region.* John Beaufoy Publishing.

Fisher, T. and N.J. Hicks. 2000. *A Photographic Guide to Birds of the Philippines.* New Holland Publishers.

Hicks, N.J. 2009. *Globetrotter Guide to the Philippines.* New Holland Publishers.

Hicks, N.J. 2010. *Presenting the Philippines.* John Beaufoy Publishing.

Hicks, N.J. 2000. *The National Parks and Other Wild Places of the Philippines.* New Holland Publishers.

Acknowledgements

The author would like to thank:

The Philippine Department of Tourism; Cathay Pacific Airways; Manila Hotel, Manila; Pan Pacific Hotel, Manila; Oxford Suites Makati Hotel, Manila; Heritage Hotel, Manila; La Laguna Beach Resort, Puerto Galera; Banaue Hotel and Youth Hostel, Banaue; Grand Season Hotel, Subic Bay; Discovery Shores Boracay Island, Boracay; Fridays Boracay, Boracay; Century 21 Hotel, Iloilo; Lagen Island Resort, El Nido; Plantation Bay, Cebu; Eskaya Resort, Bohol; ChARTs Resort Alona Beach, Bohol; Caves Dive Resort, Camiguin.

About the Author

Nigel Hicks has been a photojournalist for over 20 years. He has a vast experience of East Asia, having lived in Hong Kong and Japan for over a decade. His association with the Philippines began in the 1990s, since when he has written and photographed several books about the country.

He lives in Devon, England, with his son Jason. When not writing and photographing, he enjoys sailing his boat and wandering over his home area's coasts and hills.

Index

JOHN BEAUFOY PUBLISHING

First published in the United Kingdom in 2011 by John Beaufoy Publishing,
11 Blenheim Court, 316 Woodstock Road, Oxford OX2 7NS, England
www.johnbeaufoy.com

10 9 8 7 6 5 4 3 2

Great care has been taken to maintain the accuracy of the information contained in this work.
However, neither the publishers nor the author can be held responsible for any consequences
arising from the use of the information contained therein.

ISBN 978-1-906780-54-8

Edited, designed and typeset by Stonecastle Graphics
Cartography by William Smuts
Project management by Rosemary Wilkinson

Printed and bound in Singapore by Tien Wah Press (Pte) Ltd.

Cover captions and credits:
Back cover (left to right): *Verdant green rice terraces in northern Luzon*, © Nigel Hicks; *Floats on fishing nets on the beach at Agoho, Camiguin Island*, © Nigel Hicks; *Part of the long stretch of White Beach, Boracay*, © Nigel Hicks; *The Philippine Tarsier, 'Tarsius syrichta'*, © Nigel Hicks.

Front cover top (left to right): *The Tubbataha Reef off the coast of Palawan*, © Nigel Hicks; *The skyline of Manila Bay*, © Shutterstock.com/JJ Morales; *Catholic churches are a ubiquitous feature of the landscape*, © Shutterstock.com; *Street performers in Manila*, © Shutterstock.com/Tony Magdaraog
Front cover (centre): *The Chocolate Hills on Bohol*, © Nigel Hicks.
Front cover (bottom): *The island-hopping banca*, © Shutterstock.com/Maugli